It's a Punderful Life

I'd say this book is comparable to the work of the great humorists Molière and Wilde.

It's a Punderful Life

A fun collection of puns and wordplay

GEMMA CORRELL

I really dig these puns, man!

Yeah, groovy, baby.

DOG 'n' BONE

Published in 2014 by Dog 'n' Bone Books
An imprint of Ryland Peters & Small Ltd

20—21 Jockey's Fields   341 E 116th St
London WC1R 4BW   New York, NY 10029

www.rylandpeters.com

10 9

Text © Gemma Correll 2014
Design © Dog 'n' Bone Books 2014

A CIP catalog record for this book is available from
the Library of Congress and the British Library.

ISBN: 978 1 909313 28 6

Printed in China

Editor: Pete Jorgensen
Designer: Jerry Goldie
Illustrator: Gemma Correll

For digital editions, visit www.cicobooks.com/apps.php

THE PUNS

COMEDY GOLD

CRUSHED PINEAPPLE

A CORDIAL INVITATION

EMOTIONAL BAGGAGE

GANGSTER WRAP

DISTRESSED LEATHER

COMPLIMENTARY COLORS

MOOD SWINGS

LE PAIN

S&M&M

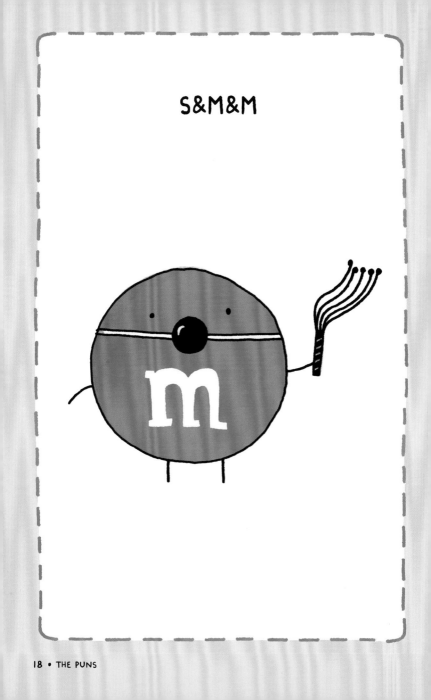

CURED MEATS

VICIOUS CYCLE

COMPLEX
CARBOHYDRATES

GLAM ROCK

PETRIFIED FOREST

ARGH!

UNRELIABLE SAUCES

SHELF AWARENESS

BLUNT PENCIL

YEAH, ACTUALLY THAT
OUTFIT DOES MAKE
YOU LOOK PRETTY FAT
I'M AFRAID.

PEAR PRESSURE

SUPPORT BRAS

BORED GAMES

SIGH.

CATAGORIZING CATS

CAT À MERINGUE

CAT À LIST

SOPHISTICATED PALETTE

WHAT'S THE PLATTER?

TRAY BIEN.

PAS TRAY BIEN.

CEREAL MONOGAMY

A PORPOISE IN LIFE

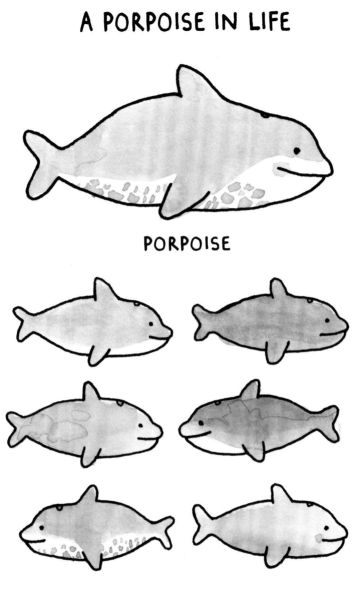

PORPOISE

MULTI PORPOISE

A CROSS DRESSER

SPOILED MILK

WORST ANEMONES

I HATE YOU!

I HATE YOU MORE!

REFINED SUGARS

HAD I THE HEAVENS' EMBROIDERED CLOTHS, ENWROUGHT WITH GOLDEN AND...

MIDDLE-AGED SPREAD

SOAP OPERA

CHILLY PEPPERS

SNAKE CHARMER

YOU ARE LOOKING *PARTICULARLY* LOVELY TODAY.

NOM DE PLUM

MATURE CHEDDAR

YOU'LL UNDERSTAND WHEN YOU'RE A GROWN UP.

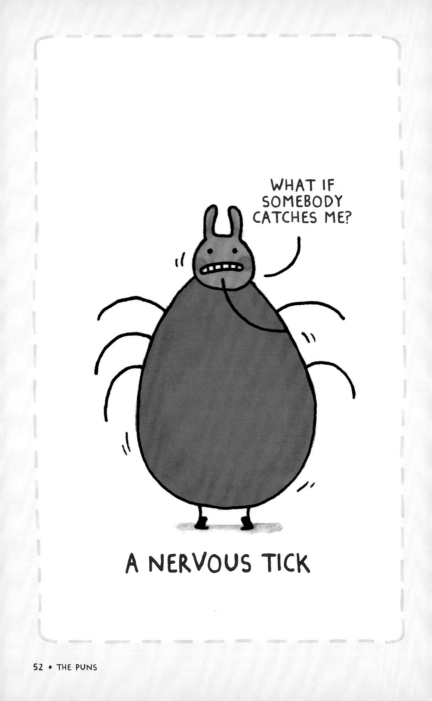

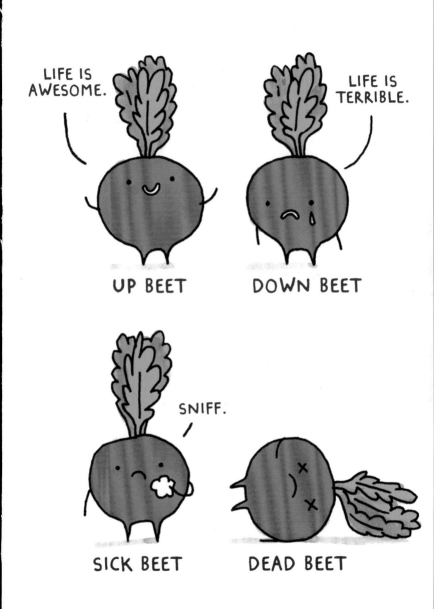

ELDERBERRIES

SENSITIVE TOOTHPASTE

MY LIFE IS
SO HARD!

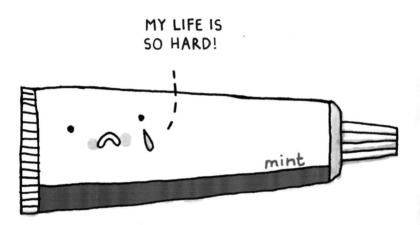

mint

ORGAN RECITAL

SEASON'S GREETINGS

A BONE TO PICK

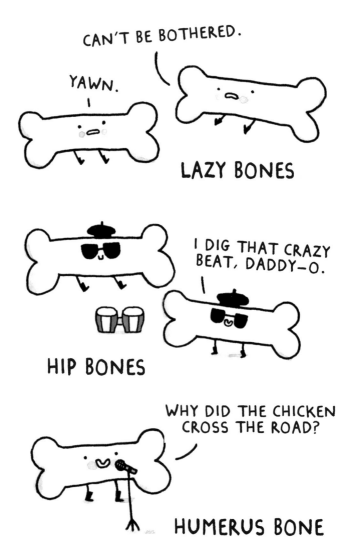

STREAKY BACON

GUT FEELINGS

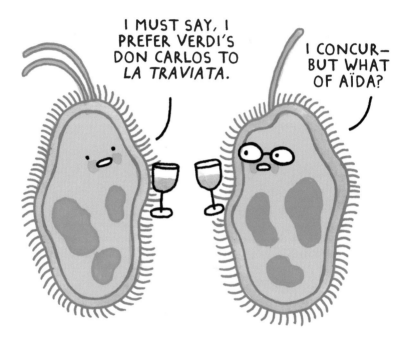

CULTURED BACTERIA

ACKNOWLEDGMENTS

I'd like to thank my friends, family and pugs for putting up with my terrible sense of humour for all these years. In particular, thank you Anthony for providing pun-related critiques and also lunch. Thank you to everybody at Dog 'n' Bone and Cico Books, especially Pete Jorgensen, and to my friends at the Red Roaster, where the coffee is never bitter.

And thank you to whoever it was that made the cuddly toy Nessies that were for sale at Pitlochry Woolen Mill in Scotland during the 1990s. "Happi-Ness", "Grumpi-Ness" and their pals continue to inspire me as I embark on my punderful journey through life.